you are a magic maker.

written by amy ferris.

illustrated by jenna stone.

ISBN:1505377013
ISBN-13:9781505377019

BOOK ONE

POST COFFEE
PRE WINE

-AMY FERRIS

DEDICATION

this book is dedicated to our moxie tribe.
you are magnificent. you are magic. you are moxie.

we love you.

amy ferris & jenna stone

you are a magic maker.

i know it's
tough out
there.
man oh
man it can
be brutal
& hard
& what feels
like the bad
is never ending.

I know there
are days
that feel endless.
hopeless.
days you wanna
throw in the towel
& give up.
i know that it can
be cruel & nasty &
sometimes plain mean.

i know that there are
days that
staying in bed,
under the covers,
hoping & praying
for night
to fall real fast
is the only prayer
you say & repeat.

but here's
THE THING:

YOU GOTTA TAKE CHARGE OF YOUR LIFE. YOU GOTTA GRAB IT SHAKE IT, AND STIR IT

YOU GOTTA STARE

LIFE SMACK IN

THE FACE

AND SAY:

YOU DON'T SCARE ME,

NOT ONE BIT,

I'M GOING AFTER WHAT I WANT.

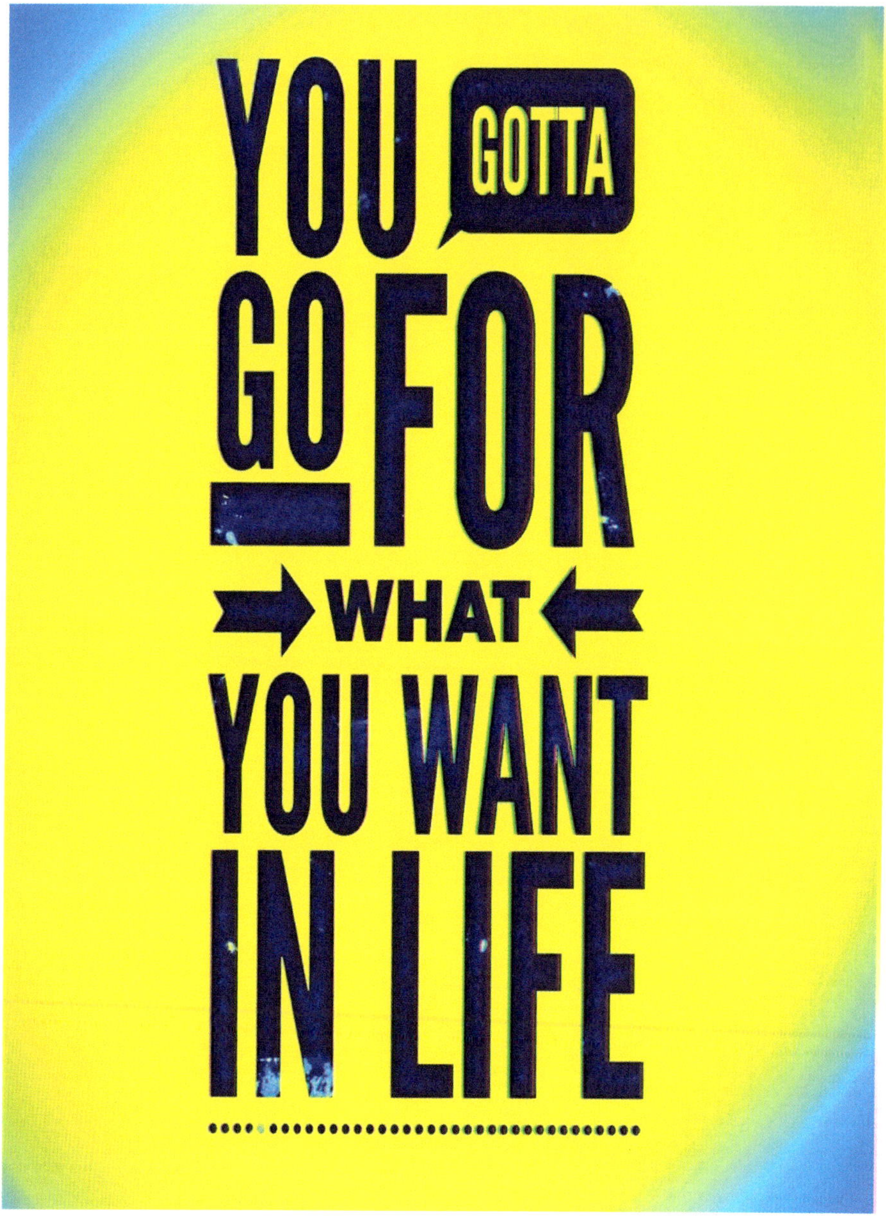
YOU GOTTA
GO FOR
WHAT
YOU WANT
IN LIFE

YOU GOTTA STOP TAKING *NO* *as an absolute.*

you gotta demand more, much more.

demand the whole enchilada,

the whole cake,

THE WHOLE SHEBANG FOR YOURSELF

AND THOSE YOU LOVE.

THE BIG,
THE SMALL,
THE TEENY,
THE HUGE,
THE
IMPOSSIBLE,

the

"this

is never gonna happen,

but i'm gonna give it

my best shot"

AND THEN SHOOT FOR

THE MOON.

and stop taking less. taking less is not noble.

YOU GOTTA STOP THINKING

THERE ISN'T ENOUGH

TO GO AROUND,

THERE IS PLENTY

TO GO AROUND,

AND A PIECE OF IT

BELONGS TO YOU.

YOU GOTTA **STOP** THINKING THAT YOUR DREAMS **AREN'T** WORTH FIGHTING FOR, OR WANTING, OR HAVING.

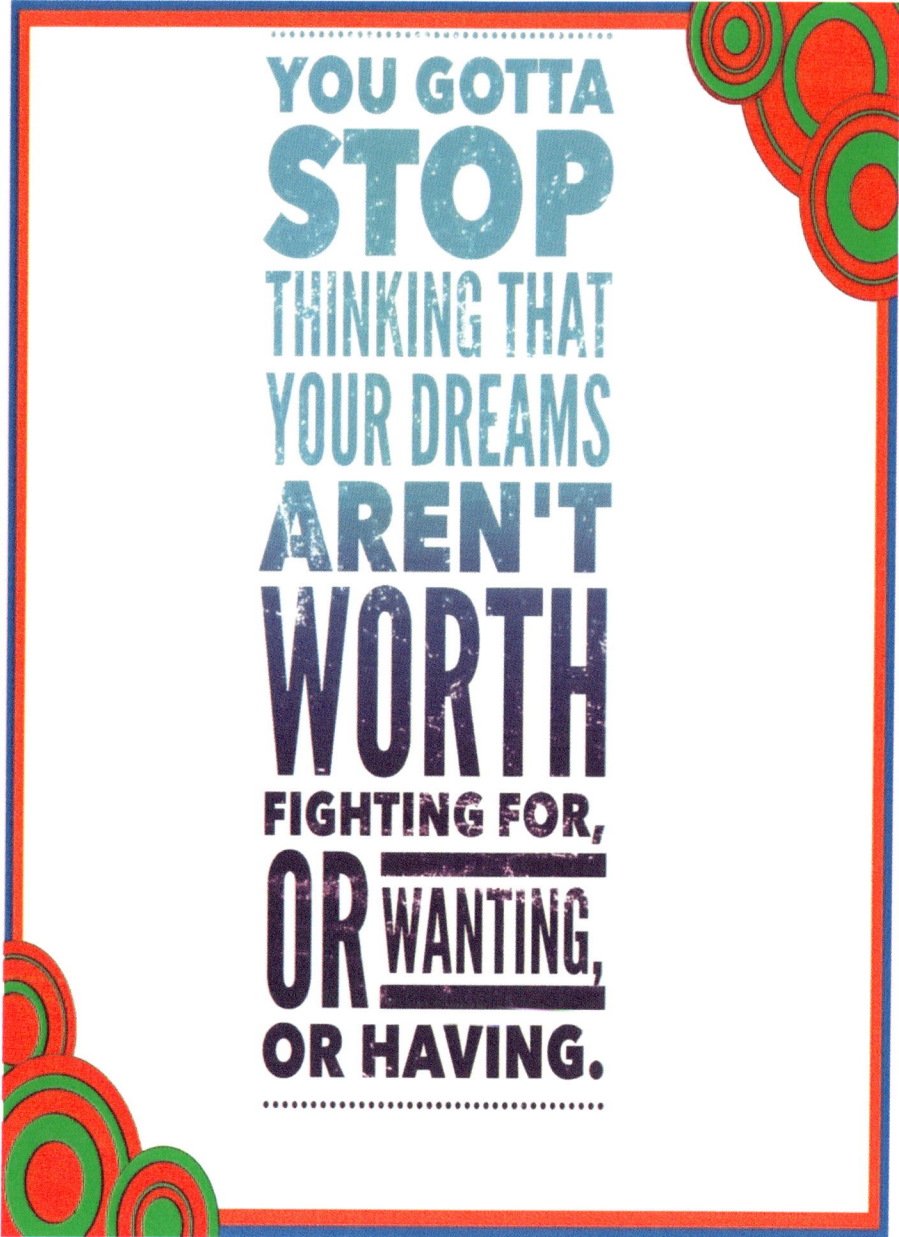

YOUR DREAMS & YOUR HOPES

& your wishes

&

your desires are what make you extraordinary,

FULFILLING THEM IS JUST THE ICING.

YOU GOTTA START BELIEVING IN YOUR GREATNESS, YOUR BEAUTY, YOUR ABSOLUTE AMAZINGNESS, YOUR TALENT, THE WORDS YOU WRITE, THE ART YOU MAKE, YOUR CREATIVITY, YOUR HEALING POWERS.

AND ALL YOU GOTTA DO
IS KEEP GOING UNTIL YOU GET THAT ONE YES.
AND IF YOU KEEP GOING,

A YES

IS ALL BUT GUARANTEED
& YOU ARE SO WORTH IT.

YOU ARE WORTH EVERY

SINGLE "NO" THAT

I PROMISE

YOU WILL TURN INTO THAT

ONE "YES"

BECAUSE ONE YES

IS ALL YOU NEED.

now go on,
TAKE THAT DREAM,
outta the drawer
AND SHAKE IT
OUT GO ON...
*shake that dream out
and try it on again.*

I'M TELLING YOU

THE WORLD NEEDS
MAGIC-MAKERS.

Amy Ferris has written a few books, a couple of movies, some television, and co-authored one off-broadway play. She was editor-in-chief of a glossy magazine, so-edited/co-created an entire women's magazine, had her own column, and co-edited an entire anthology.

She lives in a really nice house, has been married to a good, kind, cranky, awesome man for 22 years. She has some very wonderful good/great friends, a truly messed-up family, and two cats who are very sweet but not de-clawed.

She has many shoes, but no matching bags. She went through menopause, and wrote, Marrying George Clooney, Confessions From a Midlife Crisis, a funny, poignant memoir about it. She loves most foods, but believes - through incessant googling - that she is allergic to most

YOU ARE

KINDNESS. GOODNESS. GENEROSITY. FORGIVENESS. SEXY. DETERMINATION. GRACE. COMPASSION.

YOU ARE AWESOME. FIERCE & MIGHTY. YOU ARE MIRACLES, MAGIC, AND LOVE. YOU ARE IT. THE WHOLE SHEBANG.

SO GO ON AND STRUT YOUR GORGEOUS SEXY SELF. THE WORLD NEEDS YOU.
-AMY FERRIS

COLOR ME #MOXIE

www.moxiemedia.rocks

Jenna Stone